Sledding on
Hospital Hill

Sledding
on
Hospital
Hill

poems by
Leland Kinsey

DAVID R. GODINE
Publisher ❖ Boston

First published in 2003 by
DAVID R. GODINE, Publisher
Post Office Box 450
Jaffrey, New Hampshire 03452
www.godine.com

Thanks to the following magazines in which poems
of this collection have appeared:
The American Scholar: "The Flood Gives a
Millworker a Holiday"
Seven Days: "Snowmen"
North by Northeast: "The Dam Cleaners"

LIBRARY OF CONGRESS
CATALOGING-IN-PUBLICATION DATA

Kinsey, Leland
Sledding on Hospital Hill : poems /
by Leland Kinsey. — 1st ed.
p. cm.
ISBN 1-56792-224-4 (alk. paper)
I. Title
PS3561.I5737S58 2003
811'. 54—dc21   2003000005

First edition
Printed in the United States of America

Contents

Sledding on Hospital Hill

I ❖ DESCENDANTS

ERRATIC LUNCHES

My daughter and I often climb
in spring, summer, and fall,
a boulder just tall enough
to frighten her, but small
enough for her to scramble up
its angles and edges.

A glacier perched the large erratic
on the hill. Other rocks
of that same till
lie scattered thickly
over the pasture high above
a lake.
      We picnic on the narrow
top, room enough for two,
and watch the near farmer harrow
or hay his fields,
or boats plow the distant lake
with fine white furrows.

The boulder is roughly the size
and shape of an elephant.
On hot, humid days, pestered
by flies, we could pretend
that we are in the tropics
but seldom do, or that the wind
which dries our bread
will take us anywhere but here.

We see the yearly resident hawks

hover in the wind and take sparrow,
wren, cricket, mouse.

Month to month, we watch
daphne and rhodora give way
to bluet and yellow rattle, which fade
to hawkweed and steeplebush.

Today's late August.
School will take some of these times,
and her horizons will widen,
though this one's pretty huge.
I concentrate on just this place
and what she and I are doing in it,
and try not to know too often
how my words will echo
through every landscape of her life.
The crusty bread seems a luxury,
as does our ease.

PIG
LIFTING

"Pick up a pig every day from its birth
and you can do it when it's full grown,"
someone told my grandfather,
and no doubt meant the pig would let him,
but in three years my grandfather increased
his already powerful body
such that he could lift the now huge hog.

Like Milon of Croton, who lifted a calf
every day and carted it around,
and was able to lift the ox when full grown;
who won the Greek Olympics' wrestling laurel
    six times.

My grandfather did not wrestle men,
but, as a farmer, animals and the ground itself
till he was pinned by a tractor and counted out.

If he had lifted every part as made and assembled,
could he have lifted machine and death
like the pig we see in pictures
on his lap in chairs, cradled in his arms,
draped large across his back.

In my grandfather's final rendering
he could snatch nothing from old weighty death,
and left behind only scraps
like these.

SMALL WOUNDS
AND MINOR AILMENTS

Chipping my shinbone with an ax
is the first injury I remember,
standing under the Greening apple tree
on a pile of cedar slabs
at five years old trying
to split wood like my father.
The chip still floats
beneath the skin.

My father cut his hand on bottle rubble
in the pasture, a long split
at the palm base. The doctor sewed
it without anesthetic,
but it festered and bled for days.
Another doctor opened the wound
and dug the final piece of glass out.
Several nerves and tendons had been severed.
Always a man to do things in a rush,
now fine motor control
was lost in the details.

Playing gorilla in first grade
I chased the girls
and fell on a stone.
I sat outside and cried two hours,
the teacher tried to console me
then threaten me to silence.
The next morning I was taken
to the doctor, who set
my collar bone and wrapped
my arm to my chest.

Weeks later when he unwrapped
the smelly bandages
most of the skin came off my palm.
My hand felt like a weight
hitched to a string
swinging painfully, but swinging.

I chased my brother through a pasture
until he ran into
a barbed wire fence that opened
his cheek and neck.
I had not meant to hurt him
like that, but was going to fetch
him a few if I caught him.
I helped him home and caught
a few myself. Cold compresses
and carefully cut bandages
to pull the edges together
left only thin long scars
visible.

Chasing my cousin, he turned
to stick his tongue out behind
and when he turned back
he ran splat into a beam
and split his tongue three ways.
His parents had him suck on ice.
The doctor couldn't sew or tape
or bind it up. No salt,
or acidic foods, or spice,
even soda hurt. Rude pain

9

like every slapstick movie
watched on Saturday afternoons.
Humor black and sore.

In a jumping competition off the swings
at school I slipped and was clipped
in the head by the board-and-metal seat.
I bled into the sink
then in my teacher's car,
and my parents' car.
The doctor sat me on his table
and sewed my head without anesthetic,
like he had my father's hand,
with a needle like my mother used
for upholstery. He complained
I wouldn't let him shave
the whole back of my head.
Scar smile in the back of my head.

I pushed my brother in the snow
and he hit his head on a buried
plow that made a two-inch
three-cornered dent that left
a red trail to the house.
He took my threats to make
him say it was an accident
and threw them in my face.
No marks.

Forking frozen ensilage,
that I first had to chop free
and toss down the silo chute
before carrying bushels to the cows,
I drove one of the nine tines right through

my foot. I worked a while,
then went into the house
when my boot began to slosh.
I poured the blood down the sink
and asked for dry socks,
but mother said she'd finish.
I felt bad that she had
to do my work.

Building fence, pulling staples,
I drove a hammer claw
almost through my hand.
I looked at it and almost fainted
then hid it from my father,
he did not take our injuries well.
The rest of the day was hard work.

As was the day we were building
a large toolshed roof. Driving spikes
into spruce-log rafters,
I slipped and sat hard
across one poorly trimmed.
A branch stub drove into my leg
and made a hole I could stick
my thumb in. I wadded
my bandana into my pantleg
to finish out the day.

I found a thumb joint
on a bale while haying at my uncle's.
Loading the trailer for my cousins,
I found it as if set there.
I picked it up and looked around,
even at my own hand.

No grown-ups were with us.
The tractor sat idle at the backswath.
I checked again all hands around
then threw the thing away.
My mother came back
to get the piece the doctor thought
he might be able to rejoin.
I told her it was gone.
Trying to replace the shear pin
my uncle had asked my father to turn
the flywheel. He turned it wrong
and pinioned my uncle.

     It was he
who had watched his older brother
playing with a blasting cap,
and seen three fingers of his brother's hand
disappear. Unrepeatable act,
but that uncle played tricks on kids
the rest of his life
       with that hand fragment.
     That same brother shot
my uncle in the leg with his .22
when he wouldn't do his chores.

Some years later one of my cousins
was jacking the haybine
and the drawbar fell on his foot
and cleanly severed his toe.
It healed quite well
but some years later got him out of war.

When my uncle fell head-first
from his high barn roof, he caught
the ladder half-way down

and spun himself around
to land on his back.
It took him two hours to crawl
two hundred yards, and two years
in a back brace to recover.
Another failed circus act, he said.

My brother went head-first down
the hay chute, like many another,
and landed on grain bags then cement.
If his fall had not been broken
he would have been,
but he was sore for many days.

Many summers my folks did not have money
for shoes, so we children were forever stubbing
quarter-sized flaps off the ends of our toes.
We stepped on many a thing that sliced or pierced,
and sat long with our feet in pans of Epsom salts.
My brother crawled to the house
with a twisted, rusted spike stuck in his foot,
and the board it was driven through holding him back.
That two-penny nail came out with a neat S-twist.

Many months when young I suffered from barn-itch,
huge patches on my legs, and back, and chest,
and arms, but not my head to leave scars
like several of my friends. Only days before
he was killed I wouldn't let my grandfather
hold me on his lap because I did not want
him to see I was afflicted yet again.

We were often struck
by the odd names of the things we had:

Quinsy, inflammation of the tonsils
with pus-filled sores:
chilblains, sharp pains and itching
of the skin after working or walking
long in the deepest cold;
rickets, mild cases of the north,
cured by eating fish-oil capsules,
a rubbery amber pearl each day.

My father's brother married
my mother's sister and we felt
like that with those cousins.
None of us died then, or lost major
appendages. We did sprain many.
Sliding off the snowy barn roof
we hit many obstacles, and leaping
from the silo to the barn roof
we often twisted something
or caught our clothes or skin
on the heads of roofing nails,
and we were often lame
from other acts of foolishness.
From necessity and fun
we came of age knowing
we had survived. We had some
accounting of the debt we owed
and were not owed.

STEEL HYMNS

By the collapsed high drive
to my uncle's barn, which my father
had fallen through with a hayloaded truck
and drove the wheels through
the floor below into the stable
where my uncle was milking,
but the main timbers held
all from collapsing, we cousins strung
an old drive shaft on heavy copper wire
slung over an unused electric line.
We swung those five feet of fine steel
against granite outcrop foundation stones,
and what a ringing we made there.
The pealing brought our mothers first,
startled, then alarmed, then laughing.
We saw three women coming
across the wide, plowed, front fields,
stumbling some, swirling their arms.
The Crows we called them,
kept by the overseer of the poor
in long black dresses and rundown home.
When younger they had offered
themselves to men
for little down and none carried over,
because they were a little retarded
and a little lonely. Three sisters,
who came to church each Sunday,
stood below us as we rang
out our raucous chorus,
our cacophony to the tumbledown,
and sang their verses to our steel hymns.

Their notes rose clear, carried by words
indecipherable, their language
since childhood, carried like boats
on a huge swell of sound
that, if I believed, would have washed
the shores of heaven,
washed away our sins.
We were stunned, did not make fun
as they stood with their dresses heavily hemmed
by the muddy stuff of each of us.

GRANDFATHER DRESSED
BY MISSIONARIES

Each month's first Sunday's collection
supported those spreading the Word abroad,
so my parents, grandparents on mother's side,
aunts, uncles, cousins —
close and many times removed —
for that week anyway tried to tithe.
Of our fifty cows five were thus milked
and fed and tended for foreign enterprise,
as were three of grandfather's thirty.
Our stake seemed close to home
since two close women cousins taught,
and preached, and set considered example
in disparate parts of India.
One came back
from the eastern parts of over there
to visit family and gather funds.
"Arunachal Pradesh," she told us,
villages lying at the end
of some blind valley north of Assam.
She wanted to translate the gospels
into their language, "Not even Indo-European,
but Austro-Asiatic with almost no script."
Some few would shell out for that,
but she built interest by telling
how some women still had several husbands,
that tales of headhunting survived,
that the people still believed in native gods
and gods in nature. We children's poor
bare feet, iron-deficient bug eyes,
occasional case of rickets, paled

before that greater poverty of the day to day
and righteousness. Ante up.
She told some of these tales
while family sat on grandmother's porch
as the missionary dressed grandfather
in a dhoti, acreage of loincloth
smartly wrapped to baggy trousers
and little more. Grandfather stood
for pictures, his skin as white
as the cotton cloth and as pebbly
as linen from the cold.
"I believe they can be gentle people,
and we must treat them gently
but also firmly," she said.
Afterwards my favorite cousin said,
"See those knockers? What a waste."

The other missionary also returned,
from farther west. Between the two
almost the whole subcontinent spanned,
span of St. Thomas' trek.
Good sport that he was, my grandfather
also donned the livery she chose,
this time for a church supper.
After beans, and squash, and pork,
and apple and mincemeat pies,
he dressed up like a Sikh
from wrapped lower leggings
to wrapped turban. She talked
of their martial prowess,
how directly they resisted change,
had fought the Hindus and Moslems
for their place, and how strong
one must stand before them,

especially as a Christian woman,
and couldn't we see money must be spent,
for what we cousins in the back
whispered were The Missionary Wars.
In both cases grandfather later admonished
us for our "smirky ways."
Said we did not have to believe
in everything to believe someone
might do good things.

Some years later
a Naga or other one, perhaps practicing
his very old religion, or wanting
to be one of several with his wife,
parted the pacific missionary's head
from its shoulders, left the body
and took his prize for his affairs.
We had no smart remarks.

On vacation by a lake in Pakistan
the other missionary sat in a lounge
chair three years later
and took a sniper's AK-47 bullet
to the head, and it was unknown
whether she was the target or random lesson.

Especially in us children's minds
they both achieved a minor prophecy,
but we grimly failed to grant them martyrdom.

One Life's Work

Grandmother's diaries, recorded
from the age of six,
were passed down and around
at her death. The deft, small
scrawl changed little
those eighty-two years,
and her small, farming world
was surprisingly stable
while the world at large
she'd known of changed utterly.
Her little sister and trained crow
figured large in her youth.
The crow found injured in a hayfield
stayed years, stealing thimbles
they borrowed from their mother,
and the button eyes of dolls.
The girls had to cover the hens' eggs
they collected from his eyes,
though sometimes they gave him one
as reward or prize for something refound
or his croaky talk or song, price noted
only as a small egg on the page,
guilt's whole note.
She and her sister wallpapered
outbuildings her brothers built
for their sugaring, pigs, repairs,
and then abandoned to the girls,
who pretended they were houses
and schools. Once she writes
of her and her sister on their backs
papering a knee wall and under-roof

as a doll's bedroom.
She, the teacher, remarked on the smell
of crushed stems and spored leaves
as the crow and sister sat
at boulder desks in an outdoor,
ferny room. Older, she taught
for a year though never finished
high school. Dealing with the children
was easy, but she wrote her shyness
made meeting parents crushing.
She worked as teacher of the children
and house help on a farm
where she met my grandfather when he hired
out to be near school to finish.

"Father says there is a comet near,"
she wrote as nine-year-old.
"I do not know what that means
but he says he will show us."
Nights later:
"We have seen the comet. It looks
like a small moon all on fire
falling. Father says it would
do great damage should it hit,
but it doesn't seem to move.
He says it will go past in time."
This the first time her daily jottings
became a noctuary, as they became
so often later when her days
seemed ordinary, but certain nights
had wonders and unexpected turns,

which she tried to phrase right.
"After a hard day I walked with him [husband]
to the closer spring so he might drink
the water cold. I wore only
a light bedgown and would have
been ashamed for anyone but him to see,
but it felt so cool, and I walked
barefoot because the rowen
was well up. We looked down
on our land and buildings
with disbelief. We sat and lay
more restful than sleep."

Her diary states of her first child
of eight, "Baby born."
Her noctuary, several babies later,
"My children do not sleep.
I am worrisome and fumble,
but he comes and holds them only a little
while and they are quiet,
seem made well for a time if sick.
No child of ours has died (yet?),
I will not think it."

And later. "He likes to watch
me take my hair down
and brush it almost to the floor.
It is starting to turn grey.
He is as strong as ever in every way.
Will my children have to care for me
as we do my parents now?"

When grandfather was killed.
"Alone in bed for the first night

in forty-three years. I am made
to live past the death of passion.
The choirs of the church and woods
are stilled for me. "

Several brothers also kept diaries,
often just the weather facts,
but some are secreted away
by those who fear what was said,
or find family too insistent,
or feel the reflections
do not mirror the person.
To whom does anyone speak as diarist,
and how to judge. As one would music?

After her parents' 55th anniversary party
she notes in passing the instruments
her family could play: Piano, guitar,
accordion, violin, trumpet, harmonica,
pump organ, and a jew's-harp
played by a reluctant son
seen by the family as an outsider.
"A prodigal son will honor
his family in his own way.
The house came ringing full.
I do not know what I have accomplished,
but my children seem to do much well."
Eighth notes, high notes, low notes, held notes.
She had written one life's score.

Far Inland,
Listening to Ships at Sea

Home from the war with wounds
suffered on the Rhine at Remagen,
my later to be father-in-law lay
in bed many days with headphones,
listening to short-wave radio broadcasts
from large portions of the world.
When later able to farm, he strung
a long wire antenna between the house and an elm.
After chores at night he would listen,
and early in the morning, as he had listened
as his machine-gun company's radioman.
What he mostly heard were conversations
between ships, and ship to port,
all up and down the eastern seaboard.
One starry clear night
and early morning he heard the talk
as the fog-shrouded *Andrea Doria* was struck
by the *Stockholm*. The loss of life
and excitement of rescue made him feel
again the power of all he'd survived.

The army had telegraphed home
after his wounding that he was missing.
He was like Schrodinger's cat.
His mother had to feel he was dead and alive
till he was observed to be one or the other.
He'd been afraid the ship he was freighted
home in would be sunk, the same in between state.

I understood some of this
when years later he told me.
As a boy I sometimes unhooked the electric fencer
and twisted the radio antenna leads
onto the wire for a five-mile antenna
laid out on the farm's terrain.
Instead of the usual music to soothe
the cows, and baseball games
to soothe my father,
and weather reports,
I often heard what I thought was Russian,
once sputtering cries I thought
or pretended were the cosmonaut
said to be stranded,
unable to return from orbit.
I wanted him both to return
and to be the first to die in space.

In all his years of living well
nothing has been so important
to my father-in-law as three days
of being alive on his hands and wounded knees
crawling back toward his lines, toward life,
and all his life he has listened
for messages from that front.

CEDAR STILL

"Drop on the head will kill a frog,"
the man who ran the cedar still would say,
as he showed us a clear vial
of the cedar oil that he distilled.
He would then often drink,
from the return pipe, condensed vapors
containing enough of the volatile oil
to make us children think
it too was a poison he could survive.

Years later I would read how Cartier,
stranded near Cape Tourmente, Quebec,
winter-bound with his crew,
managed to survive scurvy and starvation
by brewing tea from white cedar.
Arbor vitae he named it.
The life it gave them allowed return
carrying the first North American tree
transported to the future populators.

The still-man knew white cedar well,
and red cedar, one in upland stands,
the other in boggy copses.
He pruned truckloads of twigs
to fill his huge wooden vat.
Hot and buggy work in summer.
Hotter even was any day spent
firing the arch to build steam.
The whole apparatus was built by a stream
for ready water for heating and cooling.
Hottest of all was standing

on the yet-steaming rusty-colored mass
in the vat when distilling was done.
He had to fork the whole load
over the side in order to pack
the vat again for another run.

Aristotle wrote of Greeks distilling
essential oils,
and Pliny the Elder described
distilling rosin for bows, and wax,
and, melted, for sealing ships and casks,
supplies from and for conquest,
old tricks of old invaders.

The small residue he collected
was sold for perfumes, medicines,
and household agents; not harmful at all
except in huge doses, or on the absorbent
skin of amphibians. I remember its slick
and sticky feel.

His heritage was Indian and French,
we boys' Scot, Papal versus Presbyterian.
He picked on us, and scared us,
we often tormented him,
or told our parents of the plants
he stole to sell as shrubs or hedges.

Days off school or farm work,
we often sat wide-eyed along the stream
like frogs in the heavy-scented air,
and watched him at his heavy labors,
not he nor we feeling meek, or like inheritors.

DEACON BOOZE'S SEXTON

was one of many nicknames
he endured, or only knew as mild slurs
behind his back.
He did dig graves, but for the town
not any church, and many a casket
was probably accompanied
by his empties.
He ran a sawmill for a living,
bottle in one hand, various levers
the other, and could mill true
for all he drank.
He sawed the lumber for our barn,
planed clapboards for my sister's house
and charged just enough
to keep him thick.
He had run the shingle machine
for acres of shingles, and could put
three thousand on a roof
in a day's dry work.
His barn burned and some thought fraud,
like my uncle's neighbor, who lost
barns twice and was dubbed *The Claimant*
but here it was stupor.
He threw cigarettes to neighbor boys
as he drove past in all his glorious
vehicles called *tree killers.*
Summer and winter I pulled him out
of ditches and banks, sometimes so far
off the snowy roads only the crawler
could pull him clear.

I saw his father dying of cirrhosis
lying out on their sun porch.
He lay as yellow and thin
as a slab of clear pine.
So many drunk driving citations
have been written against him
that people say, when he illegally drives,
"*Tickets* is writing another chapter."
All his equipment went past on long bed trucks
last year, but he still tells me
how many board feet he's putting
out each day.
I hope he's saved a few wide boards
to fit the hole he's dug
his whole life into.

THE FLOOD GIVES
A MILLWORKER A HOLIDAY

When the flood came
it sounded like all the clocks
in the world whirring.
My grandfather used to yell
at us a lot to get to work
but his bellow was nothing like the roar
of water taking out the bridge,
and there wasn't any work
anyone could do to save it.

It sounded like all the steam trains
were coming back through town
when the mill's heating room
went with hisses and belching
as the whole structure calved
off the rear of the great white building
like one of those icebergs
breaking into cold water
in a National Geographic special,
only the flume of flood-spray
on abutments and foundations
washed more human shores.
The guy at the hardware store gave away
most of his shovels
but there wasn't anything to be shoveled
in front of all that water.
The flood marched through town
with all the trimmings of a circus parade,
gingerbread porches and roofs
like fancy wagons, and a fine collection

of the town's wires like tinsel
and ribbon. The men on machines
trying to clear some various dams
or bridges were doing some kind of high wire,
daredevil, wing-walking act
that they didn't get paid to do.

We used to get hired to clean up
after the circus trooped through town
and we thought all those mounds
of elephant dung were too much,
but it was nothing compared
to the muck and ooze the river
left as one swath of stink.
I found out the river took Mizz Johnson
right off her porch with her own big tree,
and there was a time as a kid
I would have paid a quarter
to see her, my teacher, taken just
that way, but I'd pay a lot more
to have her put back, and my house too,
but there's no damned ticket-puncher
here to take that money.

An Old Man's Recipe
for Tongue Pickles

I am going to tell you
what one old man would not,
who told me only when he knew
I was the one who would help
him through death.

Peel and slice 3 gal. ripe cucumbers,

Big cukes, almost gone to golden.
Cut them in half lengthwise and scoop out
the seeds with a spoon,
almost like gutting a trout,
then cut across in big chunks.

Put in crock at noc.,

A kind of gardener's nocturne,
when outside work is done.
Old stoneware crocks are rare —
find one or have one made,
it will outlast you.

Add 1 cup salt and cover with water.
Drain next day, rinse if too salty.

One is reminded of the sweat
of all this enterprise.

1 pt. cider vinegar &

If you made the cider yourself
so much the better and cheaper.
I still do, then let a few gallons sit.

1 pt. H₂O to boiling.
Put about 2 qt. of cukes in kettle,
cook until they look glazey.

Till they have the shine
of an old man's rheumy eyes.

Drain and continue process.

Oldtimers call all of this *processing pickles.*

1 qt. maple syrup,

No one said it was going to be cheap,
although the old man was,
and didn't put in so much syrup
when he hadn't made it,
counting money carefully,
his own time cheap.

1 qt. vinegar,
2 pkg. dk. brown sugar.
Make a bag for the spices.
2 tsp. allspice,
½ c. pickling spice,
1 tsp. whole cloves.

He was a teacher. He brought
spices and foods into his classes

and made his students
smell and taste the conquering
of knowledge of the world,
and taught them the price of some of it.
He willed his money to pay for education.

Boil with vinegar and sugar until quite thick.

Almost like the maple syrup itself.

*Pour into crock over pickles,
let stand till they taste right.*

Which means two months at least.
The cucumber ends will look
like swollen, brown, curled tongues.
But do not think of that,
the taste is sweet with vinegar's
sharp bite on your own tongue's receptors.
His mother's pickles, whose recipe
he thought would, perhaps should,
die with him. A crock in a cool place
that holds enough for a year.
The ripe smell when fishing
the doubly ripe pieces out.
All this is your heritage now,
as it is preserved here,
make of it what you will.

Sister-in-Law

We drive the thirty miles.
So many times I've gone to find lost relatives
by car. My father's great aunt in a nursing home,
dying, telling my mother of other people dying;
trying to find my runaway cousin in Montreal,
and now I go with you to see your sister.
Signing in is the worst.
Do they know we are not sure of what it's like,
what to do, what she will do?
Ward III. She is sitting on a porch
with windows like my grandmother's bay windows,
small neat panes. She greets us, asking,
"Have you come to take me for a ride?"
"Some other day perhaps," knowing other days
will be the same because of other days.
We sit with some patients before a TV.
They cheer in monosyllables
as the windows rattle like applause,
and do not see us differently.
When the picture on the screen begins to roll,
her eyes do too; we do not watch as she looks away.
"The elm and maple seeds are falling," she says,
"but the elm trees are dying,
   and the winter salt is killing the maples," and when I
      look out
the rotting trees are loosing samaras that drift
and whirl.
            A nurse comes with medication,
and we leave as the building eclipses the sun.
You sit closer on the way back,
turning to watch the hills fall behind us,

but we cannot see what is passing.
Again and again
she is standing on the porch;
she waves, turns away, spinning away, a samara,
   one wing
extended in her rush.

MY FAMILY HORSED
AND UNHORSED

The span of white Percherons breasted
the crest of a hill
that five-year-old me had gone down
to meet them.
My uncle's young hired man rode one,
the other raced beside on a lead,
and they charged along the road
as their ancestor chargers might have
beneath a knight's heavy hand.
The same feeling rose years later
when a tractor-trailer rose before me
in my lane. Both the hired man
and driver took their charges
off the road. The semi jack-knifed,
the horses wound up thrashing,
half-swimming in a deep ditch
and came out of the stagnant ooze
blackened half-way up.
The would-be flattened one
watched precisely how others
let him survive.

My uncle had a black pair next,
bought from a man he trusted
but they had heaves.
Standing in the barn in winter
their great sides rose and fell
and they sounded like they could
have been used as blacksmith's bellows.
On green grass, outdoors each summer,
they gave good labor for a few years.

They would have done better
running out in deep cold,
but my uncle didn't know.
He sold them to the knacker
by the pound, good money
for almost two tons.

One great-great-uncle's horses
were never found when they sank
with his horseboat off the point
at a rivermouth. The continuous
cleated belt they walked
powered the ferry he ran
till it sank in a storm
and lay lost for a century.
Now it is an archeological diving
site noted on maps
where his ferry wasn't.
Some horse bones lie exposed
in the bed of the boat and lake.

A great uncle let his team walk on
with the sled-load of several thousand
board feet of timber after a branch stub
struck his eye out as he sat too high.
He said they were on an uphill
and the team never learned to lock
their legs to rest the load
so to stop was to lose the logs
and probably cut the harness
from the jumbled, injured horses.
He said he held his eye for a while,
like an ice-fisherman's bait,
but tossed it down on the glaze
when he needed his hands on the lines.

My great-grandfather packed
snow with his four-horse roller
the day after the blizzard
of '88. His first son had been born
the day of the storm.
Three miles out, beside a nearer lake,
he jumped from the high seat
to clear from before the lead team's
burlap-covered chests a drift
where they seemed to founder.
He disappeared. His brother,
riding with him, called down
into the snow hole he had made,
"Don't worry, I'll take care of the boy."
My great-grandfather always said
he didn't know how they did it,
those horses must have
been swimming in snow.

His brother moved to the city,
worked the street department teams
for years. In winter he wrangled
the two-handled scrapers
which plowed and gathered the snow
for removal. The department horses,
and those of freighters and deliverymen,
often ran away while waiting,
either startled or prodded.
"That really cleared the streets."
He remembers a milk-farm team racing
wild, and the splash of blood
on their white hocks and the snow
as the iron wheels of the wagon
cut a bystander in two.

"Not too many people killed though.
Horses looked like the racks
they trundle around in the garment district.
Drivers would hang a feed bag
while they delivered, but little enough.
Thousands of sparrows feeding
at both ends. And thousands of carcasses
to clean up each year, horses hauling
horses. People complain about junk cars,
but a car doesn't stain a place with stink
after three days. Dogs don't come
and parcel it out over a neighborhood."
Before trucks came, and he hauled
himself back home, he had liked the sound
of a powerful team clopping iron
on brick and cobblestone.

Grandfather once drove an unshod team
down off his then-iced hill.
"Two horses and enough legs for eight."
They pulled the needed hay
back up through fields of crusted snow.
He had to tend the wounds for days.

He also raced his caulk-shod horses
on frozen ponds and lakes,
snow-packed fair tracks, and broad streets.
When I drive down those streets,
I wonder how they made the turns,
but turn they did and raced for home
to pick up bets placed on the side.
My wife's grandfather did the same
and they may have raced each other,
ice shards flying in their own

and others' faces, cold echoes
of that which preceded them,
and of the competition even older
than that which brought them
to this land. In our lives
and arguments we feel
the benefits and fallout
of all those races.

Great uncle Will had to climb out
on the wagon pole to regain control
of a horse that always broke
its gait, that took the bit
in its mouth and ran. He unhitched her,
rode her around the entire mountain,
made her run a full mile
at full gallop each time she broke.
She changed her ways,
and they changed her name.

Years later a black-and-white photograph
of him going down to his horse pasture
ran in a national magazine.
His white Clydesdale stands, head turned.
The admonition *Fat is the best color*
in a horse would not apply,
though most readers would not have noted
the ripple of ribs in slant light,
or how close the grass was cropped.
Thin and slightly stooped,
my uncle stands in the background,
granite outcrops and his shirt
are white. Wraithes of their working lives,
both stare, unnoticeably blind with cataracts.

Grandfather bought the first car
in the congregation soon after
Queen (of the Mountain)'s run.
He drove it fast to church
each Sunday, as he had driven
his horses. "I like them a little
close behind," he said
of their conformation, "it lets them
gather a little more power and speed."
His own father wouldn't get out
of the way in his own buggy
when cars came up behind.
He would lead his own parade
of shiny horses and metal steeds.

My father's father had three mules
and three horses. His father worked
with a span of horses,
his older brother a pair of mules,
leaving my father a team
made up of a horse and a mule.
They pulled unevenly, the horse
was faster, the mule reluctant
to start or stop, they often fouled
his lines. Never a horseman,
when he borrowed mother's father's team
for work on our farm
he see-sawed them all over
woods and fields. It hardened their mouths,
and his heart against them.
Yet I remember their willingness
to lift heavy feet lightly
to hand or work.

As boys my father and uncle rode one horse,
not allowed to tire a team,
to baseball games each Sunday.
She would never run or trot
on the way to town, but plodded
down the long hill. They swore
and threatened to use her hide
to make more baseballs. Her pace
her own, but she had a smart
extended road-trot home.
Their horsehide dreams
carried them toward a new age.

A first cousin still logs with horses.
One winter he drew cedar
from a bog where no machinery
could go or had been
even at the height of clearing
a century before.
Some logs measured two feet
at the top cut. The horses often broke
through the frozen surface
to the muck below.
He would clean their legs and flanks;
throw small posts back across the hole
for corduroy.
The truckers who came to the landing
had laptops to compute the load.

My sister and her husband hauled
rafters for their barn
with a Morgan stallion I had broken
to harness and of many faults.

Snaking one load around a snag
he got caught up, and not knowing
how to ease off and away
he bound the load and himself tighter.
He got nervous and went over backward,
did not get too badly wither-wrung,
but they worried about making him pull
as he should. Repositioned, reattached, he cleared the
    load,
drew it and others clean all day.

It took me a year to quiet
a half-blind mare who'd been beaten
often. Her use was foaling,
but hard enough at that.
She had to be stoutly tied
for the stallion to cover her.
Trimming her hooves was more than a chore.
Once she suddenly reared,
as was her wont, and I'd been careless.
Much of her astride my back,
her front legs over my shoulders,
she rode me all the way
to the ground. "Get up,"
I said, and hoped I could;
gave a yank on the chain
I still held. She rose,
and suffered me to rise.

AFTER BIRTH

Only months after you were born
your mother's father and I took you
deep into the woods.

This sounds like the beginning
of many fairy tales I've read to you.

In the middle of a bright afternoon
we saw a moose out in the peat bog
moving to the edge where she lay down.
Through field glasses we could see
she was giving birth, her flanks heaving
then long slow pushes. We watched the hooves
and then the face emerge still in the amnion.
I held you to the window to see some of this.

You were too young to understand,
but I told you I would tell you.

I could not help but think of your birth.
Your mother pushed for eight hours
before the doctor cut a new smile
and pulled you back up the canal
and out, and the force of pushing
had shaped your head like the moose calf's snout.

I am writing this in part to tell you,
and to fathom once again the waves
of emotion in all of this.

The moose licked her calf
while the afterbirth hung from her
then fell.

The doctor was just beginning
to draw out your afterbirth
when I left your mother to go
with you, your face was still
a worrisome blue and you had swallowed
some of your meconium.

Your grandfather and I could see
a young moose near the channel,
probably the one just abandoned
for new birth.

Your hand clenched
mine as they worked on you.
As you grew pink I could look at you
as solid and lasting, and brushed
from your forehead already long dark hair.
I held you then, pure animal
wanting only food and drink,
and wished to give you all the best
parts of the world your mother and I knew,
and knew even with the years we had
we would fail.

Your blood is part of the blood
on the operating room floor.
You have tasted shit, taste wonder.
Find places like a remote northern bog
for wonder. Live fairly happily
for a fairly long time.

CRIES IN THE NIGHT

was my mock-horror description
of what we would hear.
I took my daughter owling
in late deep winter
as I did my son.
We camped by a peat bog
surrounded by a mountain, two hills,
and one long ridge.
I woke her mid-night to walk out
and hear the mating calls of owls.
The barred owl's eight part song
sounds like a distant hound
baying after deer.
Easy to imitate, we called one in.
It moved closer with each answer
until its answer was two parted
and standing.
The saw-whet's cry is just
what anyone who has set the teeth
of a saw then sent a file along the edge
of each to sharpen them has heard.
The loggers who first cleared
this entire landscape now covered
with second growth, and they with ground,
would have heard their own whetting
winter long, but the saw-whet's imitation
is only a three month's song.
The great horned owl's booming hoot
can be heard across the good sized
territory it will claim,

and anything smaller must beware,
great horned owls breed early
so all the spring's young
can be their fare.
A rare boreal owl's voice
is what we think of as owl,
a melodious hoo-hooing in deep woods.
The screech owl's cry is the sound track
of B-horror flicks, and my daughter flinches
when it cuts the quiet.
The coyotes on the ridge were also voicing,
a sound she had heard in cowboy films
but that seemed closer, louder, here.
In the day we had seen blood on the snow
where, from the tracks, two had mated,
I did not know if it was from ovulation,
or the anteing-up of submission.
There was no child whimpering
or baby's blat of bear calls,
distressingly human to human ears,
as the bears still hibernated,
though my daughter feared and longed for
their ambling out.

　　Nights like this may play back
　　in her mind when boys bay at her
　　in ways both foolish and profound.

She and I stand slightly shivering
trying to enlarge our hemisphere of hearing.

SNOWMEN

When I worked weekends
so visitations were mid-week,
my boy and I often made snowmen
after school. At these latitudes
after school in winter is night.
We hulked huge torsos together
taller than me so that I had to lift him
onto my shoulders to put heads on theirs.
We stabbed in a whole mittened hand
for O-gape mouths,
used coal from the cellar for eyes,
though the house was thirty years on oil.
From the hay mower in the aging carriage barn
we took rusty cutter bar guards for noses,
pointy steel proboscises
that warm skin would stick to.
We stuck straw in them for old age hairs,
sometimes a little sometimes more,
plus wads in the ears. Apple-branch arms
from winter's pruning hung akimbo.

If my wife was willing
I would have her come out
with camera and flash to take pictures
of snowmen silhouetted against deep winter night.
With unreflective eyes and hollow shadow mouths,
wearing my grandfathers' pie caps or fedoras,
the snowmen in the photos stand, or sit,
or drive great white cars we also made,
and somewhere beside one or among several
my son's and my white faces — eyes red, our
     mouths agape,
I guess with laughter.

II ❖ It's All Work

SURVIVING BULLS

The whitewashed walls were smeared with blood
the day the bull rampaged inside the barn
after escaping from its pen.
My father gave my brother and me
each a stout stick to block exits
and hoped we didn't have to use them
as he beat the bull around the stable floor,
bloodied its nose, dented his ribs,
as the bull had done to my mother
when it pinned her to the ground
in the pasture and rolled and butted her about.
He'd then gone in the barn with the cows
and she managed to crawl beyond the fence
where we found her sitting when we came
home from the fields.

I once had a young Jersey bull turn on me
in the muddy barnyard.
He came from the side, lowered his horns
and bowled me over cleanly
and two or three of his feet tromped
me into the mud. I struggled up
and he turned to come again.
I pulled a fence post from the ground
and laid it hard right on his crown.
He went down to his knees
recovered and fled to the woods
with me in pursuit
and not until a half-mile in
did I notice I still carried the heavy post.

A full grown Holstein bull charged me once
with no chance for escape.
I jumped slightly as he hit,
wrapped my legs around his nose,
my arms around his neck
and gave a twist that took him down
heavily but not much on me
and stunned him enough to give me time to run.

My brother, not so lucky, was rumpled good
by the same bull in an open field,
held at the chest by the bull's head
as the bull spun round
then backed up for more,
but my brother sprung behind
a lone utility pole
and after a short savage dance
the bull walked off, and my brother,
breathing painfully, walked home.

The snap once broke on the nose ring pole
as my father led an Ayrshire bull to breed.
In the tight enclosure the bull knocked
my father about and down like a skittle peg,
but he rolled under a high enough board
and got away with a bruised leg,
and an unwanted lesson in maintenance.

My father had taken nothing out on that bull,
but this day he gave the bull who knocked

my mother down a hard and useless lesson.
After it all he called the commission sales
to come and get the bull while it still stood,
and gave my swollen, black-and-blue mother
the check to cash and spend in town,
but she just put it by.

Weeds

My family often went out
to deal with weeds in ditches
and waste places.
                    Some
my parents hated to see:

Even in her Sunday clothes
my mother would stop to pull bed straw,
invader of fields and pastures,
hauling it out in great handfuls
furiously so we wouldn't be late.

Father or I mowed our roadsides
once a summer as the law demanded,
and I loved the clack of the cutter bar
and the rattle of the pitmans
as the ripe ragweed was scythed low.

We pulled wild cucumber vines off hedges
and fence line trees. We children used
its prickly fruit as ammunition,
the spines inoculating us
to certain kinds of pain.

On those same fence rows hops grew,
one of many plants that served
as harbingers of welcome
times, but still of work.
We collected the dried ripe cones
to sell to the hop man for making beer
though mother hated any alcohol.

Rare in our climate, sassafras was sought
for its root bark. The aromatic oil,

thought a panacea, now thought
carcinogenic, was once shipped
by the ton to Europe. It cured
our thirst as root beer, the mild fermentations
coming to a head in our cellar.

We gathered coltsfoot, known since Roman times,
herbalists' shop sign. We dried it
for smoking to help with asthma;
made yellow candies for winter coughs
and sore throats; crushed the leaves
in honey to sooth our wounds
as it had soothed those of legions
two millennia before, anti-bacterial
before it was known they existed.

Dandelions grew large
at the gravelly edge
of roads, the dust easily washed off.
We boiled the leaves and buds
with a chunk of side meat
and ate them with vinegar as a favored green.

Wild asparagus abounded on sunny banks,
Our short knives went slip, slip.
We piled it high on buttered toast for breakfast.

We dug chicory root to cut
coffee with as they had in the war,
though then it was prompted
by scarcity of coffee, later of cash.

We gathered tansy, word derived
from the Greek for immortality, to boil

the yellow-button heads and lacey leaves
for a drink to fight us children's worms,
and for a dish called *tansy*,
with eggs, and cream, the juice of herbs,
baked in a pewter pan brought from Scotland
almost two centuries before.

We picked heavily amidst the ruderal
of old cellarholes and barn foundations:
raspberries to can, or to reduce the juice
for shrub; blackberries the same;
currants and gooseberries, where allowed
to stand so they wouldn't kill the pines
with rust, we kids stripped from the bushes
and ate plain, the almost painful tang,
before saving enough for pies;
the long white roots of horseradish
dug and pulled feet deep
with one's own feet planted wide
for the slow tug of discovery,
later the scrubbing clean
and grinding up of these tear-inducing
earthy spines worse than onions.

Which reminds me of the wild leeks
we loosed from loamy soil, and cooked, and ate
too many of, distressing goodness.

We partook or disposed of all these crops
that seeded themselves
into our history. I see us
often bent, hands invisible in the pungent
abundance at the edge of things.

DUGOUTS

For a time my brother and I fashioned
dugouts in several places about the farm.
With our father's pick and two old spades

we dug small square rooms.
Any furniture was made
of immovable outcroppings. Traced

on the walls, runic signs.
Over the dugouts we carefully placed
sticks, boards, boughs, sod,

to disguise them, and hid them
well enough so once a heifer trod
onto one and fell through.

We were not in it, and she wasn't long,
scrambling up our trued
walls with difficulty. Our father stood

akimbo, surveying our almost subterranean
abode, laughed and said we would
have to stop setting traps about.

We learned that he himself had built
versions of such childhood redoubts
on his mother's land.

A runaway lake of local history
had deposited deep beds of sand
that he dug shelters in. Shale

was what my brother and I mostly quarried.
The thin topsoil was a frail
structure from which to depend a farm.

Why we dug I do not know, stories
of breastworks or trenches, or fearing harm
from atomic bombs, or some of all

these things; and our father
listening on the radio to bombs fall
on London, and news of bunkers.

Any of this I suppose would make
children want to hunker
down, dig down. Grandmother's hired man, disgusted,

had buried his old pickup in a sand pit.
We boys wanted to dig down to its rusted
hulk and have at once vehicle and place.

When mother read us the myths,
we thought how fun to race
to old Hades' door in a Ford V-8,

and after going so far down,
turn and spin hot rocks at Fate,
rise completely up, and laugh about surviving.

State engineers drilled test holes
for rebuilding a nearby bridge for arriving
lumber-laden trucks, found a dozen feet

of hardpan over sixty of flowing sand
left by the huge lake from the glaciers' retreat.
They said they couldn't pump the casing

clear to find bedrock. We didn't care
to dig any more. The earth had seem embracing,
now seemed as fluid and insubstantial as the air.

Children Sledding
on Hospital Hill

Children are sliding on an open bank
and snow-packed lawn sloping down from city hospital.
No single path defines the run,
and too many riders coming down for one trail anyway,
so paths criss-cross with mostly no collisions.
Only plastic sleds are allowed,
and sitting is the rule,
but little kids are passed by teen-age galoots
and the brightly colored runnerless sleds slewing
gives it all a carnival, bumper-car air,
as do the cries at near-misses and thumps.

As a boy my parents once took
me to Cottage Hospital in town
to see my grandfather bed-bound
from an operation. I remember the yellow
room and his sallow skin.
I had brought my sled
because father knew they closed
a side street by the recovery wing.
After my hellos, I took my steel-runnered
Flyer down, and down, and down
that perfectly snow-compacted street
as smooth and wrinkle free as a starched sheet.
I passed almost every kid I raced.
I grabbed some runners and skidded the kids
or flipped them off, a few bumped heads
and ice-scrubbed faces. No crying,
this was the game as it was played,
no pushing and shoving in the trudge back up,

61

though sometimes a punch or two,
but mostly preparing for the next run.
I didn't know these kids
but knew the rules. I slid
till the lights came on
in my grandfather's room.
My folks and I rode home in an icy night
so cold the roads weren't slippery.

My wife is in city hospital
to see if our unborn child will be all right,
and I am out here watching our son slide.
With fear and pleasure I watch him make
his wild careenings.

PELTING WASP AND HORNET NESTS

Grey, stiff paper wrapped
carefully around the egg comb
attached to trees and buildings
was often our target.
We farm children had been stung many times,
crying, swearing, swatting hard
when climbing in attics, or trees,
or under shed rafters.
We learned to follow
the fat-bodied hornets — yellow, black,
white-striped — or the narrow-waisted
wasps — blue, black, green,
dull orange — back to their nests.
We would then pelt them
with what was at hand,
stones, or green or ripe apples.
  Apples were often these insects' food.
  They swarmed around apple cider pomace
  dumped after the pressings,
    or a single apple eaten in hand.
We flung those hard missiles
at and through the stiff sides
of nests that sounded like paper bags
collapsing. And we ran like hell
as the protective hordes homed
in on us. We would try to lead
that angry train to our safety,
a door or deep water. Sometimes stings
and welts taught us to pitch better,
farther, but our small hatred
would not let those beings be.

FERRYING TRACTORS

Starting at my father's farm
ferrying tractors to my uncle's
five miles away, I passed
fifteen farms including theirs.

One large farm carried a hundred milkers
plus young stock replacements.
Its high drive spanned the road
like a bridge from well kept fields
to the yawning four story mows.
Huge loads often rode above me.

A French family scrabbled along
with rented cows on rented land
for most of my youth.
Half of the fifteen children at least
would run to the road as I passed,
huge wheels flying, full on the gas.
Their father still used horses
and all of their backs even more
than my father and uncle used us.

One old man and his wife,
whose barn was mostly fallen in
and the house going from one end,
kept his three cows on poor pasture
by tying sap bucket covers
over their eyes so they would not see
unkept fences and the truer green.
I often stopped to shoo them from the road.
The wife would pass out candies to us kids

if we gave her a ride to town in the car,
and we thanked her, but mother
would never allow us to eat it.

A Seventh Day Adventist owned
one former farm of my family.
Neighbors said it meant he took
six days off and worked little on the seventh.
Funds were raised by all
when his daughter impaled her eye
on a spike careless carpentry
left exposed by a door. They saved the eye
for looks but she couldn't look through it.
I often waved at her pale face in a window.

Most of the farms kept the families all right,
with sugaring and winter logging
and all the attendant tractor wrangling
to fill out the checks.
Now crops of houses grow
on the best fields close to town,
almost as many as before the Civil War.
Milkweed, grey birch, and poplars
seed many others my family cleared,
and no machinery makes its noise or gains.

If I were to drive those miles
today in any fashion
thirteen farms have disappeared,
including my father's and uncle's.

❖   ❖   ❖

Sugaring, plowing, harrowing, planting, haying,
spraying, corn chopping waited to be done in a rush.
Except for cold winter days and storms,
when the tractor had to be ferried no matter,
often below zero the gas lines
had to be cleared of ice, the small knurled knobs
bitter on the hands, the flash
of evaporation when gas washed over them
instantly turned them white and frost burned,
the chill shakes for an hour before the fire
after arrival to restore me for the drive home,
or the time scrap steel tore the rear tire open
and the ballast fountained
over everything as I raced on,
a pinwheel of chloride spray,
I used to enjoy the break from work.
I knew the road's ruts and washboards,
every frost, and culvert, heave;
summer and winter the deepest ditches
from which I'd pull the odd traveller;
the steepest hill where I would kick
the tractor out of gear loaded or not
and let it run down full tilt,
life or death be damned for the thrill;
the tractor's front end danced around
and lifted on that same hill as I hauled
overloaded corn trailers, the rear wheels spitting
and grabbing as they chewed —
the brakes wouldn't hold if I stopped —
and me pulling back on the steering wheel
as if to aide the pull,
ready to jump and pretend I could make it
if the tractor finally seemed it would not.

I knew every shady copse,
every brook, and each would draw
my eyes away from what immediately mattered,
the chatter of wheels on gravel
or chains on ice,
the sense of speed in all
the world that I knew passing.

BLACK MARKS

As young men, we slapped
those old Fords and Chevys
into reverse at forty, tromped
on the pedal and the squeal would rise
in pitch and intensity
as the smoke rose grey then black
and the stink would hit as hard
as the sound of the tires.
The clunk of the automatic trans
rushed you forward in your seat
all the way through the teardrop
rip and cake on the pavement.
Our fathers' tires were worn
and shredded by designs
and straight ahead runs.

Once Warner blew the engine of his 409 Merc
after laying down a *year*,
a 365-foot tread mark
not including the three-foot
blank as he shifted first to second
in the column-mounted three.
He drifted off into an unditched cornfield,
road-smoke and steam around him.
The V-finned hulk sat as monument
to foolish technique for three weeks
before the local wreckage shop
hauled it south to salvage parts
for others' hot-rod stunts.

I drove backroads with a spray
of dirt and rocky shrapnel at every corner.
The hail-like damage to flowers and vegetables
angered neighbors and frightened cows; no
    car-chasing dogs
dared try. My grandfather, too, was cursed
for his speeding ways. But it all seemed
like farmyard stuff till the tread bit blacktop
and whatever races began to unfold.

We wrenched new heads
onto Plymouth hemis, reworked ratios
on Fireflights, drove to new heights
in Strato-Cruisers, jammed our fingers
on push-button automatics, explored
the red-line mysteries
on DeSotos' rising-grid speedometers.

We old boys held our fingers tightly in the indents
of those plastic steering wheels,
our faces distorted in the bright chrome rings,
our left elbows cool but braced on the window ledges
of coupes and sedans driven past
watching girls sometimes, or competition,
or often our own stakes and markers, but always
    driven past
capability and sense, hoping, without hoping,
something might emerge from the dirt, and smoke,
    and mirrors,
something like our full-blown lives.

69

BENONI

My son and his friends are beating
apples from a tree beyond the pasture.
The tree is a Benoni, popular
for eating out of hand for many years,
but fruit not large enough to be commercial
so now all but absent from the catalogues
and land. My grandfather grafted this one,
as all named species must be
except the original sport branch or tree,
his precise whip graft sealed with his recipe
of resin, beeswax, and rendered tallow,
and I am somewhat loathe to see
the long maple whips strike hard
to clear it of its wormy fruit
for the sport of boys, but I let them.
Besides pitching them at each other,
they slice them onto their bike spokes
till each is a spindle of apple turnings
for a kind of decoration
like roses in a parade.

                    Rosaceae,
apples a branch in the rose family tree,
chance division long ago.
Benoni, name Rachel gave her son
as she lay dying, given often
to a motherless child,
fitting for that Dedham, Mass. mutation.

The boys' method of harvest is an old one.
Olive trees are still beaten of their fruit

in all their orchards, the fruit
then gathered in stippled light.
Long wielded sticks still strike walnuts
from the tallest trees. Juglone
produced in the walnut roots
will kill apple trees and others,
a self-protective herbicide.

          The damage
the boys inflict on branches and bark
makes me recoil even more
from the old saying:
Women, dogs, and walnut trees
all benefit from a beating.
Many a thing has been stripped
by a hard swung rod divining
the unnecessary, and the necessary.

The day happens to be fine.
This minor savagery caught my eye
and as I watch my child I am glad
to let that wonderous chance
meeting of genes and molecules beat on.

Luminescence by the Breakwater

My wife, our children, I
  walked below the tideline
one October night.
  By drift pools along the spine

of granite blocks on this rock-ribbed
  shore, and at each
little running edge of sea and sand
  on this three-mile beach,

flecks of light like chisel
  sparks sparked.
When our boy said he saw light sizzle
  in the dark,

we didn't at first believe him.
  He danced, laughed
in a depression, wouldn't come.
  I gaffed

him with my arm, lifted him
  and where he'd
stood his footprints lasted,
  outlined by beads

of microscopic light, hundreds,
  thousands, tens
of thousands, depending on pressure,
  of radial diadems

of phosphorescence. The fossil sand,
  diatomaceous earth,
was awash and lighted by its own
  descendants' birth.

The waves' weight, ours, our splashing hands,
  caused the irridescence
at each force's edge, ripples
  illuminating presence.

My children's feet were neon signs
  flashing as they sped
headlong into the night. Their hands
  held galaxies, red

shifted as they moved away. Who would
  ever guess descent
of all this life from original flinders
  become radiant.

WRITING AT THE STATE HOSPITAL

A red chimney one hundred fifty feet tall
abides above all the brick edifices.
Its gentle purpose, to vent huge boilers
which heat all these abodes
for the mentally infirm,
is undermined by history's pictograph.
I entered the grounds by the East Gate,
unlocked the rotunda which housed
the library each Monday for months
to teach writing to those who cared
to try.

One old man's yellow leisure suit stood out
at hospital and in town,
where he was allowed to wander free
after twenty-two years locked up.
Warm months in the day he resided
at the railway station.
"Listen close," he'd nod at the rails,
"You can hear one coming. Going
to be a Big BANG." Such laughter.
He had tried when young to undermine
a viaduct that carried trains
across a river's rapids
because a train had carried
off his departing love.
He now drew trains in great detail
on paper, sometimes sheets so long
he had to roll them up. Sacred scrolls.
He even used dozens of punched paper

rolls from a player piano donated
long ago, the night music they then enfolded
resonant but largely silent,
like steam trains in a diesel age
chuffing no doubt toward some unseen
catastrophe, and he the cartulary
of doomsayers' promises and predictions.
His exploits had been chronicled
in a book of state railway disasters,
so he walked among the ordinary,
watched and whispered about
more as a kind of American hero
than threat, a Jesse James of love.

The sane shall build
for the insane
to see them well
or not again.

Verse from a locked-ward member
who claimed to have heard it
or made it up depending on the moment.
He liked his cigarettes
like inmates and patients and staff alike
who all kept the rooms dressed in blue.

Cigarettes
I love my cigarettes
they help me eat
and to forget

I love drinking
beer with my family
when they see
and talk to me

I love smoking with my girl
before and after
sex that makes me forget
my family's laughter.

I last saw him in a boarding home.
"Which do you think is more important,"
he said, "to get an idol, a wife, or a trainee?"
"Which do you need more?"
"I want a wife, and if I got a wife
I would mean it, but if I had a wife
I would need a trainee so I could be
a builder of houses. An idol
is important too, like John Lennon,
he has a wife, he is an idol.
If I had a wife, she could be a trainee
and be on stage with me. Do you think?"
"Would you still want to build?"
"Yes, the hippies have learned from others,
and they are builders of houses."
I thought of ramshackle shacks
scattered in raw places. I left
him sitting in an ill-lit, panelled room
dreaming of getting an idol, a wife,
and a trainee.
        I had tried for one,
maybe two, but was none of the three.

❖   ❖   ❖

76

The children's ward was hardest to enter
though the easiest of access, and brightest.

  A tall lanky boy, admitted by his family
because he kept small dead birds
under his pillow and killed mice
to feed the dead, wrote
of the talon-torn, talon-born,
and methods of protection and escape.
A fat boy, who stole the family food,
and from neighborhood stores and gardens,
described feasts monarchs would envy:
venison, grouse, grouse eggs,
roast heron stuffed with butternuts,
trout and morels, or lions' manes,
apple crisp with cheddar cheese,
his father's wines, dandelion, chokecherry.
A nervous boy with folded hands
ran to me each time I arrived
to ask always the same two questions.
"Do you like me?" and after I said, "Yes."
"Is that a little sad?"
                    I would say, "No."

"Perspicacity!" said the gaunt, straight,
elderly woman who liked to strike
fresh men across the face,
and all men were fresh.
I kept my distance and suggested
walks at imminent moments.
The one word answered my question
about what she wanted in her writing.
I had never to that point
in college or life heard the word

used right, and she questioned
whether I knew its meaning.
I assured her I knew
but that I didn't always
achieve it in my life or writing.
She smiled. She was sometimes
on the locked ward, sometimes the open.

A heavy woman on the locked ward
said, "Aren't you a tall piece
of something delicious. Have you seen
one of these?" and lifted her shirt
to show a breast. "Or two together?"
and revealed the other.
Before she could lower her shirt
she was ushered off to solitary.
Her usher and attendant attended school
in my class before she entered
a kind of nymphomania,
followed by a hard apprenticeship
served on that same floor. She serves
the rough and fragile alike
with kindness but no sympathy.

Separate buildings were reached
by underground tunnels
which seemed as elaborate,
well-supplied, and defensible
as Gibraltar, but in dusky
corners where water seeped
and where dusty shelves held contents
undecipherable they seemed
not passageways but catacombs,
an image that fit with the stories

existing of death and bodies.
Stories more riveting than most written
in my classes.
            A small man
on the locked ward who liked to talk
of penises and anuses told of a boy
on the children's ward who wouldn't talk,
kept as a catamite by an orderly
who trained him to crawl through heating ducts
to any vent where he'd left candy,
then killed him in his teens
when the boy decided to talk to girls.
The desiccated body impedes flow
through the ducts to chilly rooms.
  By the tales, more children had been born
to patients than existed in the hospital
and town, though likely some pregnancies
were less than immaculate.
                  I did meet
three Jesus Christs, and his father
once. Only one had ever done
any carpentry, another had grown older
than the last books written,
the other was contemplating suicide
but figured he'd have to change
his scriptures. He smiled and asked
if I'd criticize those, if he brought
in the revisions. "Well,"
I said, "You want them memorable."

A woman looking out at the unmarked grounds
and huge dying elms one early winter evening
said, "Don't those trees look
like wrought-iron balconies,

and the city has been freshly painted
for the revelries."

❖   ❖   ❖

Two great tomes came in the door.
Of all the writers' faces
I remember these the least,
the works seem like manuscripts on legs.
The novel was written on ledgers
housed in insurance company folders,
dumpster finds. The man had been to war
but his face was ageless
and I never knew which war,
though his part had been in Asia.
"I have two orphans placed in America.
A soldier wants to keep track of them,
but one's in the Rockies,
one's in the East. This is not for technical
purposes of the novel, the man is deeply
troubled by their fate. He has knowledge
of the orphans' families but fears
injuring the orphans by telling them,
and getting the families injured
by his contact. He has lost several
families, and wants a huge
extended one to call his own.
I've written from the orphans'
point of view, because they know
or come to know both cultures.
That's my point. I don't know
if I can make it. Make it plain."
"Can I see it? I'll help you
let the story do it."
"I can't write here.

I tried at the half-way house
but they're half-ways assholes.
I tried at my sister's
but she wants me to work."
Work never did proceed
but the drinking did.
He blamed himself for the death of JFK
because he had been drunk on the day
of the assassination.
I told him that was presumptuous,
and thought it remarkable.
  The other great work stood
as two long columns page after page.
The left-hand column explained
the writer's feelings about every thing
that had occurred that he had knowledge of
during his life span. "I used
some things my parents told me,
because my mind is just a great big filter."
The right-hand column reported every fact
and detail responded to. The columns
could also be read straight across
and made as much sense as any other way.
"It's funny how you think you understand
something or someone, and . . ." he paused,
put two fingers up, then suddenly
twisted them hard. "I don't know
how to put it into words."
This work came back to me
in a contest I judged. He had expanded
it to include geologic time
and much of history, all events
whose randomness might have led
to him.

He was living in the ruins
of a huge scale factory, and made jokes
when I met him about weighing his life.
He won the prize, and not from sympathy.

Beebe was thirty-seven, a graduate
of the children's ward, then approaching
thirty years inside in all.
He never faced the person he was addressing,
but turned his whole body to the side
and mumbled what sounded like nonsense.
He did not write the first few times
he came, but Williams' "To Waken an Old Lady"
awakened this in him:

> *Old age is a flight of small birds*
> *They wind and forfat the air*
> *They bell worm and chichel in the evening air*
> *They bite and stit in the evening air*
> *fields saw where*
> *they gripe and inpindle chat or windl*
> *Ellion blamsparble & they anche it up*

The all-but-untutored syntax orderly
with language like lonely twins
sometimes create, but here the nouns
and verbs both clarify and obfuscate.
Another time I tried to read he said,
  "You needn't always begin
from such a high level of language."
He said it face on and loud.
His hands moved
every second he was awake.
When I pressed him once,

he explained, "I'm building
a window for my father to look through."
Weeks later he raised one of those hands
to vote with the majority
to end all sessions.

.

III ❖ THE DAM CLEANERS

THE DAM CLEANERS

The dam let open
water falls where fish once climbed.
Small arcs of light lie over white,
willow trees' toothed simple leaves drip
in the new heavy rising mist.
The men wait the days-long wait
for the water to lower in order
that they begin to scrape and drag
the long neglected bed and dam.
The men who will do the work return
to the mill, their houses, fields, and mines.
From any one of five surrounding hills
the sound of falling water falling
is as clear as if standing right beside it;
the drought-lowered river cannot resupply
the pond. These few summer nights
few lights   the power grid not great enough
to supply their use. People, urged to let
the farmers have their needs,
fall back on almost forgotten arts:
talk, remembrance, noting dull aches,
and hates, and imagining desire
satisfied. Before mothers and daughters
call them home children and the old
take pleasure in standing on the shore
no longer a shore, and watching the new edge
shorten toward a darkness deeper
than any they want to know; before the clambor
of calls each dusk they wait to see the bottom
cobbled with a town's small history,

and each makes his own inventory
of
    WHAT IS REVEALED,
and some will know and some invent
the reason for each thing's being there.
The long braces of a covered bridge
in the queen post style
stand up first, brought down
in the flood of nineteen-twenty-seven
when the cleared, soil-slipped,
sheep-pastured hills could not hold
the once in a century torrents of November.
And some could now place this certain bridge
but it was only one of many
that left roads dangling as markers
in the flood's high water.
They were the old swept down,
the new as well, the lower four stories
of the first steel beam building
in the Northeast Kingdom,
angle braced and riveted
by young men learning a trade
that was booming
in the cities they dreamed of moving to
    and climbing over, but here
the unsettled granite foundation
shifted on its flood-fouled footings
and lowered this frame
higher than a church steeple
to nestle against the dam's back face,
both skeletons familiar
because of pale silver images
flickering in a public television documentary
on the greatest disaster

in the state's human memory.
The railroad bridge built high
over the gorge escaped, but the rails
were cut in fifteen places
and two box cars on their sides
open their doors again to light.
Washed from the siding by the mill,
they hold half loads of white pine lumber.
One 1927 Franklin   the aluminum
of its chassis and engine uncorroded,
its laminated ash frame long since gone.
"Doctor was within sight of his house and died,
found him wedged in a culvert
his linen duster starched with mud."
Tires, some of the first and last things seen,
those with words on their treads
to those with rusting cable steel.
Tydol cans, Mobil's red horse
once more exposed to air
and a faint hint of Atlantic Oil.
Elixer, beer, and extract bottles.
Sunk in the slime a local inventor's
ice cutting machine that worked
till it sank and he made others
and saved many a horse's life.
"They used to fall through
and we'd try to hold their reins
but they'd panic and flail at the ice
with their calked hooves and weaken.
Sometimes you could grapple them out
with another team, even then they'd die.
We tried to save the harness though."
The unbleached bones protruding
do not have leather girdling them.

89

One child's skull is seen
before the pack of licensed dogs
playing and fighting in the mud
find it too and cart it up main street
bringing the small horror of the thing itself
and people chasing after.
Speculation spreading about which family's
child's child was lost or cast,
whose abortion, natural or designed, preceded,
probably came to one or more who knew,
no facts spread.
The skull was tossed like a softball back
down the river's throat.
Edges of small bone utensils,
chips of chert and flint
unnoticed in the gravel wear away.
Red salamanders slide
from where the water left them
into the narrowing clouded surface,
they one of the voiceless notes
in

    THE SALIENTIAN NIGHT.
Noise of the last vocal hylas dissipates,
the crucifix on their backs ironic
when they're threaded on snelled hooks
leaded to lower them to brook trout feeding.
Green, pickerel, leopard frogs lose
weedy beds and camouflage
and for months after the bull frog
population will be so low that red flannel
on a string will not in an afternoon
catch a meal, their low, old-man harrumphs missed,
their delicate legs longed for.
Even toads in dark leaf mold will thin

from the lack of insect breeding shallows,
one short duration generation washed down,
becoming part of
           THE UNSEEN, UNHEARD, OR GONE.
The muskrats try to stick it out
in rush houses now open to predators —
cattail eating mats dry.
In abandoned muskrat houses snapping turtles
sink lower in the hardening ooze,
their crayfish prey is deeper
than they care to go, they'll wait the rise,
this artificial extension of drought
no different to their simple minds
than the real thing but more of them will feel
the dull thud of broomsticks
on their backs and a shovel
prying up fresh soup meat
as the sediment bank makes wide
and easy hunting possible.
The deeper-swimming wood turtle
is seldom caught or sought,
in its prime the most handsome species
but time wears away its carapace,
brittle pieces like oiled coral sinking.
And spent spinners whirl on down
while imitation hatches hover,
careful casting lands a specimen lightly,
almost dragless watched carefully
from above by a dry-fly fisherman
from below by the few remaining squaretails
in gravel pockets and boulder eddies,
the slow backwater edging the rapid.
Now and then in daylight and in moonlight
orange flesh and a thick green back

are pulled clear or seen as one more
falling body where its relatives
the landlocked salmon rose
BEFORE THE DAM
After the one great dam
and its many advancing and retreating arms
carried its load of Arctic ice, and char,
far south and blocked every northern
north flowing river in the world
and stocked them, melted, left
huge freshwater lakes, melted further
and raised the oceans' level
and marine life moved over once dry
now rebounding land that caused the feeding basin
of each river to raise its mouth from the sea
and what the cut off arms left captured
mostly did not survive except the salmon
that even in fresh water made runs
from the lakes to breed in mountain streams.
The people who followed the sea
and its shore and walked through this valley
following walrus, seals, whales,
the edge of their likelihood
thousands of years before
those who first lived here —
but all had seen the spit and curl and drive
of landlocked salmon up the falls —
had stood on the orbicular granite intrusion
and speared their winter meat,
the atlatl used for caribou and mammoth
unnecessary here, but the hands
that fashioned birdstones dominated
what they sought to dominate.
They did not match the fury of farmers,

who early in this century stood
with pitchforks at the foot of
THE NEW-MADE DAM.
Accountants, diarists kept track.
"First kilowatts of electricity produced
this month. Approx. thirty thousand fish destroyed."
"Husband brought home wagonload of salmon,
ate and salted what we could, buried the rest
in the garden for fertilizer. Remembered
the Indians taught the Pilgrims
to plant fish with their corn."
The dam that was built to run the mill
began to run the town, people's lives
prospered and eased, paid a dependable wage.
Seventeen teams went out each day
each with its high-wheeled donkey,
each cutter assigned to return that night
with a bole of full-length hardwood.
Where a makeshift dam had only penned logs
and powered a wheeled drag saw,
this turbined one fused men to machines
that shaved wood to the finest veneer.
It was a thing to watch
a thing to drive for miles to see.
One could walk the gangway
to the middle of the dam and feel
the turbines hum, and when the even light
filled the streets and homes at evening
there was a fastness to each being's
sense of being. Now for only the second time
the dam is ready for
A CLEANING
of its cracked face and silted racks and holding pond.
A drag line crane and small bulldozer

work the solid edge. Out near the channel
where the bottom's gone only horses
and scrapers can go and return
so the last teams in the area
are hired and trucked down.
Two men are assigned each team,
a driver and one to handle the handled scraper,
a useful tool from the century gone.
The festival begins. A few kids slide
like otters on the open ooze,
the men feel the jar of the scrapers'
edges on unexpected angles.
Cannon and hock deep in flat mud
the horses move, clotted hooves
give little traction, workers and teams fall often
to their knees in work's prayer.
Men have walked easier on the moon,
the terrain remote, the effect of light similar.
The job is to move the silt to the drag,
renew the bed, clear the penstock
and turbine racks for a clean unchecked flow,
patch the checks and hairline fractures.
So while some haul silt and rock flour
others trowel fine mix Portland stone.
The new pours after the flood
did not adhere well in the gapes
or to abutments left standing
and the shifting turbine torn steel rods
still stick out like sundials.
Some remember the time of pulling
the old turbine from its blocks.
Every team the veneer mill owned lined up
and straining at the shaft and vanes
shifted and broken by water alone

94

and that which it carried when it leapt
the lip and cascaded in a golden dome.
As truck after truck of sediment leaves
the back of the dam appears to rise,
a battlement that serves its servants well.
This is hubbub   this is as it needs to be,
no one is concerned or pays attention
to the
        BIRDS DISTURBED.
The bittern's hummocked nest near the inlet
would still provide protection
but the recluse is gone,
his pumping piledriver voice absented
from the mechanical overlay of sound.
Kingfishers' purview spoiled,
from tree limb perches the river's a ribbon,
below them only the occasional squirm
of bullpout in summer hibernation,
no all night tire burning fishing bouts
to bring them up to squeak,
and flop, and fry.
The halcyon nests, dug in banks,
are easily found by raccoons.
Ducklings and mother safer from foxes
have no slow water
in which to dabble nailed bills.
Heron stalk the few remaining frogs
and rifle the slumping lillies for seed,
boys with BB guns shoot
at the heron's secretarial plumes,
a fashion prerequisite of great-grandmothers,
but the dated game brings slow death.
The glancing beak of a wounded great blue
could split a millboard down its roughsawn spine.

95

Spotted and lesser sandpipers bob and dip
on sandbanks in a widened domain.
The resident Cooper's hawk has to drown
its prey in faster water,
squirrels, starlings, barnyard fowl
now made heavier by the turbulence,
like the mackinaw of a hated man
trussed up and tossed in years ago.
His hawk nose the only thing broken
as he rode the penstock toward his death
watched by the men who'd thrown him.
Despite the local newspaper's rewards
people shut up for life.
Kingbirds flash backs the color of rolled steel
and nightjars bend their wings at dusk
in patterns only they could bend them to.
Above nor below the dam
the nitrogen-crystal silver sides of fish
are no longer darkened
by the sudden osprey's shadow.
One morning, the last work done,
the future secured for a time,
THE RISE BEGINS
                    to cover again the houses once razed,
the roads abandoned, the trysting spots
of the oldest lovers. The water is a poor mirror.
Able to reflect Pisces and Aquarius faintly,
it is sun warmed, neutrino transduced,
transported and impounded,
curling back toward the observer's eye
like a memory of his origins.
The people find themselves longing for rain,
for wet and definite cover;
longing to believe that they have held back nothing.

96

SLEDDING ON HOSPITAL HILL

has been set in a digital version of Matthew Carter's Galliard, a type introduced by the Mergenthaler Linotype Company in 1978 under the direction of Mike Parker. Based on the types created by Robert Granjon in the sixteenth century, Galliard is the first of its genre to be designed exclusively for phototypesetting. At the time Carter started work on his new type, Granjon's work was little recognized among designers; his italics had been co-opted as partners for the Garamond types and his romans heavily reworked under the name Plantin. Rather than attempt a literal copy of a particular type, Carter sought to capture the spirit of a Granjon original, and in so doing created a type with a distinct heft and a dense color on the page, and a sparkle not found in most Garamond revivals.

Design and composition by
Susan H. Sims